FASZINATION NORDSEE

AUS DER LUFT FOTOGRAFIERT VON MARTIN ELSEN

IMPRESSUM

Herausgeber:	MCE Verlag
Redaktion:	Peter von Allwörden
Fotos:	Martin Elsen, Stade
Titel, Layout und Satz:	Herwig Baak, Stade
Übersetzung:	Speakeasy Communication, Emer Lettow
Druck:	creaktiv print + more
ISBN:	9783938097359
Verlag:	© 2015 MCE Verlagsgesellschaft mbH & Co. KG (Medien Contor Elbe), Sietwender Straße 73, 21706 Drochtersen www.mce-verlag.de, Tel. 0 41 43 435

IMPRINT

Published by:	MCE Verlag
Editing:	Peter von Allwörden
Photos:	Martin Elsen, Stade
Title, layout and typesetting:	Herwig Baak, Stade
Translation:	Speakeasy Communication, Emer Lettow
Print:	creaktiv print + more
ISBN:	9783938097359
Publisher:	© 2015 MCE Verlagsgesellschaft mbH & Co. KG (Medien Contor Elbe), Sietwender Straße 73, 21706 Drochtersen, Germany, www.mce-verlag.de, Tel. +49 4143 435

FASZINATION NORDSEE

DIE DEUTSCHE NORDSEEKÜSTE MIT DEN FLÜSSEN ELBE UND WESER

AUS DER LUFT FOTOGRAFIERT VON MARTIN ELSEN

INHALT

WINDPARK NÖRDLICH VON BRUNSBÜTTEL
WIND FARM NORTH OF BRUNSBUETTEL

AIRBUS-WERK IN FINKENWERDER MIT EINEM A380
AN A380 AT THE AIRBUS PLANT IN FINKENWERDER

TAKE OFF

Aus der Luft hat man gewöhnlich eine ganze andere Sicht auf die Dinge, eine andere Perspektive eben. Um solche anderen Perspektiven und besonderen Blickwinkel geht es in diesem Bildband.

Der Bildband umfasst das Gebiet der gesamten deutschen Nordseeküste von der niederländischen bis zur dänischen Grenze mit den Inseln, aber auch mit den großen Flussregionen von Elbe und Weser bis hin zur Weltmetropole und Hafenstadt Hamburg.

Gegliedert ist der Bildband in folgende Abschnitte:

- Ostfriesische Küste und Inseln
- Jadebusen und Weser: Von Wilhelmshaven bis Bremerhaven und Bremen
- Deutsche Bucht und Elbe: Von Cuxhaven bis Hamburg
- Nordfriesische Küste und Inseln

„Von oben" seine eigene Heimat wahrzunehmen, ist oft ein spannender Prozess. Wir wünschen viel Spaß beim Schauen und Entdecken.

Ihr MCE Verlag

One normally views things very differently, has a different perspective, from the air. This collection of photographs deals with precisely that other perspective and special view.

The collection encompasses the entire North Sea Coastal region from the Dutch to the Danish border, including the islands and the great river regions of the Elbe and Weser as well as the world metropolis and harbour city of Hamburg.

The collection is divided into the following sections:

- East Friesian coast and islands
- Jadebusen and Weser: From Wilhelmshaven to Bremerhaven and Bremen
- German Bight and Elbe: From Cuxhaven to Hamburg
- North Friesian coast and islands

"From above" perceiving one's own home is often an exciting process. We wish you a great deal of pleasure in looking at the pictures and in discovering the region.

Your MCE Verlag

NORD-OSTSEE-KANAL MIT HOCHBRÜCKE (44 METER HÖHE), BRUNSBÜTTEL
KIEL CANAL WITH HIGH BRIDGE (44 METERS) BRUNSBUETTEL

NORDSEE-KÜSTE

EIN WIRTSCHAFTS- UND LEBENSRAUM

Wir Norddeutsche leben in einer wundervollen Umgebung und haben das große Glück, diese auch zu jeder Zeit genießen zu dürfen. Die Nordsee und die Elbe prägen unsere Region, die sich über Jahrhunderte in maritimer Verbundenheit entwickelt hat. Zugegeben, einem selber ist oft gar nicht bewusst, was für imposante Landschaften sich im näheren Umkreis finden lassen.

Martin Elsen, der seit Jahren eine feste Größe im Bereich der Landschafts- und Luftbildfotografie ist, stellt in diesem Werk eine Auswahl der eindrucksvollsten Ansichten aus der Vogelperspektive dar und gibt dem Leser damit ein Gefühl für die Schönheit der norddeutschen Küstenregion. Die detailreichen Darstellungen zeigen, wie sich Natur und Wirtschaft vereinen und wie Arbeit und Erholung direkt miteinander verbunden sind.

Damit eine Region stark wird, muss viel Arbeit geleistet werden, damit sie stark bleibt, muss sehr viel mehr Arbeit investiert werden. Standortfaktoren wie qualitativ hochwertiger Wohnraum, Nahversorgung, Bildung und Kinderbetreuung und vor allem auch attraktive Arbeitsplätze spielen heute im Wettbewerb um den Faktor Mensch eine große und bedeutsame Rolle. Damit kleinere Städte und Gemeinden auch zukünftig attraktiv für junge Fachkräfte sind, müssen die öffentliche Hand, Kammern und Verbände und die Unternehmen Hand in Hand arbeiten.

Als Beispiel für so eine übergreifende Zusammenarbeit soll an dieser Stelle ein kurzer Blick auf den Standort Stade gerichtet werden. Die wirtschaftliche Entwicklung der Hansestadt Stade zeigt deutlich, dass Stade mehr als nur ein Mittelzentrum ist. Von besonderer Bedeutung ist einerseits die Entwicklung der Unternehmen an der Elbe, insbesondere auch die Hafenentwicklung, andererseits der Ausbau der Verkehrsinfrastruktur. Die Hansestadt Stade ist integraler Bestandteil der Metropolregion Hamburg und des Wirtschaftsraums Unterelbe.

Zukünftig wird das Wachstum bei fortschreitender Globalisierung an den Standorten liegen, an denen Logistik und Produktion zusammenkommen und optimiert werden können. Die Chancen, die sich aus einer regionalen Zusammenarbeit und Bündelung der Kompetenzen im Unterelberaum ergeben, müssen im Wettbewerb mit den großen Seehäfen der Welt genutzt werden. Dabei sind unsere Wettbewerber nicht die anderen deutschen Häfen in Niedersachsen, Bremen oder Hamburg. Der Seehafen Stade ist im Verbund mit den Seaports of Niedersachsen und den Elbe Seaports gewachsen, die Arbeit nimmt in allen Bereichen an Qualität zu.

Ein Teil der in diesem Buch gezeigten Bilder zeigt, wie sich die Hansestadt Stade am Elbufer in die Landschaft integriert hat: die historische Altstadt, die neueren Wohnstandorte außerhalb des Stadtkerns, die Verkehrsanbindung sowie die Industrie im Norden und Süden der Stadt. Großunternehmen wie die Dow, Airbus oder die AOS Stade geben als Industriegrößen vielen Menschen Arbeit und sorgen für Wohlstand. Dies wiederum führt zur Ansiedlung von jungen Menschen, die das Stadtleben bereichern und dafür sorgen, dass Stade einer gesunden Zukunft entgegenblickt.

Oft ist es die Perspektive, die eine Fotografie für den Betrachter zu etwas Besonderem macht. Nicht viel anders ist es mit unserer Nordseeküste. Neue ungewöhnliche Blickwinkel ermöglichen auch eine neue Wahrnehmung der Region. Besonders spektakulär ist dabei der Blick von oben auf Nordseeküste und Elbe. Hier werden die Ähnlichkeit der Landschaft, die Siedlungs- und auch die Wirtschaftsstrukturen besonders deutlich. Administrative Grenzen, wie sie in der Realität für viele von uns täglich wahrnehmbar sind, spielen hier keine Rolle. Im Gegenteil: die Gemeinsamkeiten der Region, ihre Geschlossenheit treten in den Vordergrund. So ist aus dieser Perspektive auch die Elbe nicht mehr als das trennende Element wahrzunehmen. Vielmehr wird ihre Bedeutung als zentrale und verbindende Wirtschafts- und Verkehrsachse offensichtlich.

Nordseeküste und Elbe bestimmen eben nicht nur unser Klima und das Landschaftsbild. Sie ermöglichen einen florierenden Tourismus, bieten umweltfreundliche Transportmöglichkeiten, versorgen die Region mit vielfältigen Gütern und bieten letztlich zahlreiche Arbeitsplätze. Sie machen die Region zu etwas Besonderem und in jeder Hinsicht liebens- und lebenswert.

Die Häfen sind dabei die wirtschaftlichen Drehscheiben. Über sie laufen die internationalen Warenimporte und -exporte. Ihre Bedeutung hat durch die Globalisierung erheblich zugenommen und wird auch weiter zunehmen. Hierin liegt eine große Chance für die Unterelberegion und die gesamte Nordseeküste. Verarbeitendes Gewerbe mit hoher Ex- und Importabhängigkeit ist zunehmend auf umweltfreundliche, zuverlässige und zugleich kostengünstige Transportmöglichkeiten angewiesen. Der Seeverkehr stellt hierbei eine optimale Lösung dar. Die Nordseeküste bietet in Verbindung mit der Elbe für diese Unternehmen optimale Standortbedingungen und der Region damit hervorragende Entwicklungsperspektiven.

Die Akteure der Region arbeiten daran und schaffen es zunehmend besser, trennende Elemente zu überwinden und die Gemeinsamkeiten weiterzuentwickeln. Neben dem gemeinsamen länderübergreifenden Engagement in der Metropolregion Hamburg gibt es inzwischen zahlreiche weitere Kooperationen – etwa zwischen den Seehäfen oder den Unternehmen beiderseits der Elbe. Einhergehend mit dem dringend erforderlichen Ausbau der Verkehrsinfrastruktur wird das Transportnetz weiter zusammenwachsen und wird sich die Kooperation noch verstärken.

Nordseeküste und Elbe bieten Lebensqualität, hochqualifizierte und motivierte Menschen, viele Standortvorteile für Unternehmen und damit insgesamt hervorragende wirtschaftliche Entwicklungsperspektiven.

Die Fotografien in diesem Bildband können dabei helfen, den erforderlichen Sichtwechsel auf die Nordseeküste zu vollziehen, ermöglichen sie uns doch den Blick auf das eindrucksvolle große Ganze und machen Lust, die Region mit ihren Menschen unmittelbar vor Ort zu erleben – vielleicht als Besucher, vielleicht aber auch als neuer Unternehmer oder Bewohner der Nordseeküste.

Marco Dibbern
Wirtschaftsförderung der Hansestadt Stade und Standortmanager des Seehafen Stade e.V.

Martin Bockler
IHK Stade für den Elbe-Weser-Raum

HALLIG NORDEROOG
HALLIG NORDEROOG

NORTH SEA COAST

A COMMERCIAL AND RESIDENTIAL AREA

We northern Germans live in a wonderful environment and are lucky enough to be able to enjoy it at any time. The North Sea and the Elbe shape our region, which has developed along with its maritime bond over centuries. Admittedly, we ourselves are not always conscious of the impressive landscapes surrounding us.

In this work, Martin Elsen, who has been a constant of landscape and aerial photography for many years, portrays a selection of his most impressive birds-eye-views, giving the reader a feeling for the beauty of the Northern German Coastal Region. The detailed illustrations demonstrate how commerce and nature combine, and how work and relaxation are interconnected.

A lot of work needs to be done in order for a region to become strong. For it to remain strong, much more work needs to be invested. Location factors such as high-quality living areas, food supply, education, childcare and, above all, attractive workplaces play a large and meaningful role in the competition for the "human factor". The public sector, chambers, associations and companies must work hand in hand to ensure that young towns and villages are also attractive for young specialists in the future.

For an example of such inter-cooperation, it is worth taking a glance at Stade. The commercial development of the Hansestadt (Hanseatic City) Stade clearly demonstrates that Stade is far more than a mere mid-sized town. The development of the companies on the Elbe is especially important, particularly the harbour development, as is the expansion of the transport infrastructure. The Hansestadt Stade is an integral part of the Hamburg Metropolitan Region and the Unterelbe commercial area.

In the future, with ever progressing globalisation, growth will be seen in locations where logistics and production meet and can be optimised. The opportunities arising from regional cooperation and the bundeling of competencies in the Unterelbe area must be grasped while competing with the great sea harbours of the world. Our competitors are not the other German maritime harbours in Lower Saxony, Bremen or Hamburg. The maritime harbour in Stade has grown in association with the Seaports of Niedersachsen (Lower Saxony) and the Elbe Seaports. The quality of the work is improving steadily in all areas.

Some of the pictures in this book demonstrate how the Hansestadt Stade has integrated with the nature along the Elbe banks: the historic old town, the newer residential areas outside the city centre, the transport links as well as the industry in the north and south of the city. Major concerns such as Dow, Airbus and AOS Stade provide employment for many people, thus contributing to prosperity. This in turn attracts young people, who enrich city life and ensure that Stade has a healthy future to look forward to.

It is often the perspective of a photograph that makes it special to the beholder. Our North Sea Coast is no different. New, unusual perspectives enable a new perception of the region. The aerial view of the North Sea Coast and Elbe is especially spectacular, whereby the similarities in the landscape, and the residential and commercial structures become especially clear. Administrative boundaries, as we perceive them day-to-day, are of no consequence here. On the contrary: the similarities in the region and its closeness come to the fore. Thus, from this perspective, the Elbe can no longer be viewed as a separating element. Rather, its importance as the central and unifying commercial and transport corridor becomes obvious.

The North Sea Coast and Elbe not only define our climate and landscape but also contribute to flourishing tourism, offer environmentally friendly transport possibilities, supply us with all manner of goods and offer the region numerous jobs. They make the region special and above all lovable and well worth living in. Thus, the harbours are commercial hubs. International goods imports and exports are carried out through these harbours. Their importance has increased considerably due to globalisation and will continue to increase. This provides a great opportunity to the Unterelbe region and the entire North Sea Coast. Manufacturing industry, which is highly dependent on exporting and importing goods, is increasingly reliant on environmentally friendly, reliable and also economical transportation methods. In this case, sea transport offers the optimum solution. The North Sea Coast, in connection with the Elbe river, is the optimum location for such companies, and as such offers excellent development perspectives for the region.

Those active for the region are working on, and achieving their goal of overcoming divisive factors and further developing commonalities. Apart from the common, cross-border activities in the Hamburg Metropolitan Region, there are now numerous other co-operations – as between the sea harbours or companies on both sides of the Elbe. Along with the much-needed infrastructural development, the transport network will continue to grow together and cooperation will be reinforced. The North Sea Coast and Elbe offer quality of life, highly qualified and motivated people, numerous location advantages for companies and thus, in total excellent commercial development possibilities.

The photographs in this collection can help achieve the necessary change in perception of the North Sea Coast and allow us to view the impressive area in its entirety while awakening the desire to experience the region and its people directly – perhaps as visitors, perhaps as new entrepreneurs or citizens of the North Sea Coast.

Marco Dibbern
Wirtschaftsförderung der Hansestadt Stade
(Stade Economic Development)
and Location Manager of the Seehafen Stade e.V.

Martin Bockler
IHK (Chamber of Commerce and Industry) Stade for the Elbe-Weser Region

DAS WATTENMEER

NATURRAUM VON WELTWEITER BEDEUTUNG

Perspektivwechsel sind für uns Menschen oft notwendig, um etwas Neues erleben und wahrnehmen zu können. Die Bilder von Martin Elsen bieten uns diesen Wechsel, liefern uns ganz neue Eindrücke, Sicht- und Seh-Weisen von unserer Umwelt direkt nebenan – in Bildern, die wir so nicht kennen und oft so noch nie gesehen haben.

Das Wattenmeer braucht auch einen Perspektivwechsel, will man es begreifen: Den meisten Menschen ist der Lebensraum Wattenmeer nur vom Deich aus bekannt: endlose Weite vor der Wurster Küste, bei Niedrigwasser bräunlich-grau. Die großen Priele erscheinen als Lebensadern. Bewegt man sich ins Watt hinein, begleitet von einem Nationalpark-Wattführer, erfährt man die Details im Kleinen: Sandhaufen des Wattwurms, Atemlöcher der Muscheln oder die zarten Kratzspuren der Schlickkrebse, die mit ihren Antennen ein filigranes, wenngleich nur millimetergroßes Muster in die Schlickoberfläche zeichnen.
Das Wattenmeer aus der Luft bietet hingegen etwas völlig anderes: die Weite erfährt eine neue Dimension, denn sie ist nicht eintönig oder gleichartig, sondern durchsetzt von großen oder kleinen oder tausendfach kleinsten Prielen, die ein ganz eigenes Muster bilden, für die Be- und Entwässerung der Wattrücken, für das Lebenselixier des Watts, das Nordseewasser. Diese Muster sind nur auf dem Foto stabil. In der Natur verändern sie ihr Gesicht von Tag zu Tag. Im kurzen Zeitrahmen nur minimal, auf ein Menschenleben gerechnet verändern sich Priele und Watten, Inseln und Salzwiesen deutlich, oft erkennt man es nicht wieder.
Das Wattenmeer vor unserer Küste – von den Niederlanden bis hinaus nach Dänemark – ist einzigartig in der Welt: so groß, so unzerschnitten, so jung und so dynamisch gibt es eine solche Landschaft nirgendwo auf der Welt. Die UNESCO hat im Jahre 2009 entschieden, dass das Wattenmeer in das Weltnaturerbe der Menschheit aufgenommen wird, als ein unverzichtbarer Bestandteil unserer Umwelt für die gesamte Menschheit in Verantwortung bei uns vor der gesamten Menschheit. Eine hohe Auszeichnung und Anerkennung, aber auch eine große Aufgabe für die, die für den Schutz Verantwortung tragen.
Millionen von Schlickkrebsen, Wattwürmern oder Muscheln charakterisieren die Biologie des Wattenmeeres, Tierarten, die in besonderer Weise in der Lage sind, den Widrigkeiten des Lebensraumes zu trotzen: den Tiden, den damit einhergehenden Temperatur-, Salzgehalts-, Strömungs- oder Lichtintensitätsschwankungen. Sie haben Strategien entwickelt, dennoch zu überleben und tun dies in sehr hoher Anzahl, denn jede Tide und

DIE AUSSENWESER
THE OUTER WESER

die Zuflüsse in das Wattenmeer, die Elbe, Weser, Ems oder Jade bringen beständig Nahrung für diese Tiere, sodass extrem hohe Populationsdichten erreicht werden, ein Schlaraffenland! So wurden mehr als 100 000 Schlickkrebse auf einem Quadratmeter Watt gezählt. Dies ist dann die Grundlage für die weiteren Glieder in der Nahrungskette des Wattenmeeres, vor allem für Zugvögel und Meeressäuger wie den Seehund.

Das Wattenmeer braucht wie kaum ein anderer Lebensraum den Perspektivwechsel, wozu dieser prachtvolle Bildband einlädt und eine besondere Sichtweise offenbart. Wir Menschen lassen uns von diesem Naturraum faszinieren: Hunderttausende gehen alljährlich ins Watt, Hunderttausende besuchen alljährlich die Nationalpark-Häuser, Millionen von Gästen kommen zu uns wegen dieser besonderen Natur und der weitaus überwiegende Teil dieser Menschen wünscht sich einen aktiven und gut organisierten Schutz der Natur, damit uns diese Besonderheiten erhalten bleiben. Der Naturschutz am Wattenmeer erfährt heute eine ganz außergewöhnliche Unterstützung bei den Menschen, die hier Urlaub machen und bei den Menschen, die hier leben und arbeiten, weil sie genau wissen, dass ein lebenswertes Umfeld Voraussetzung und Notwendigkeit für ein erfolgreiches Gemeinschaftsleben ist.

Natur und Mensch zusammen zu führen, ist in einem Raum wie dem Wattenmeer oder an der Unterelbe noch viel mehr Voraussetzung für ein gutes Leben der Menschen und Zukunftssicherung für einen guten Schutz der Natur. Und die Bilder von Martin Elsen machen auch dies besonders deutlich, wie eng verzahnt Wirtschaft und Natur in diesem Raum sind. Oftmals stoßen beide „Welten“ unmittelbar und ungebremst aufeinander und der Betrachter spürt die Spannung, die zwischen beiden Seiten besteht. Die eine Seite charakterisiert wirtschaftliche Prosperität, die andere qualifiziert ein lebenswertes Umfeld, was auch für das menschliche soziale Miteinander von einer zunehmenden Bedeutung ist und geradezu essenziell für viele Ansiedlungswillige in Zeiten des demografischen Wandels. Insofern steht unser Raum auch dafür, die Brücken zwischen den beiden scheinbar entgegengesetzt wirkenden Sphären von Natur und Wirtschaft zu bauen und mit Leben zu füllen. Auch für diese Brücken gibt es an unserer Wattenmeerküste gute Beispiele. So grenzt der Containerhafen Bremerhaven direkt und unmittelbar an den Nationalpark Niedersächsisches Wattenmeer. Mit diesem Schutzgebiet wurde 1986 das gesamte Wattenmeer vor der niedersächsischen Küste geschützt, was wesentliche Voraussetzung für die Aufnahme des Gebietes in das Weltnaturerbe war.

Im Zuge des Containerhafenbaus wurden Ersatzmaßnahmen umgesetzt, die im Nationalpark zu mehr Wattenmeer-Natur geführt haben, ehemalige Sommerpolder wurden renaturiert und zu wertvollen Räumen für die Wattenmeervögel und -pflanzen entwickelt. Neben dem starken Eingriff in die Weserwatten durch den Hafenbau konnte so aber ein erheblicher Gewinn für das Wattenmeer geschafft werden. Dies gelingt nur, wenn die Menschen von der Sinnhaftigkeit solcher Maßnahmen überzeugt werden, wenn sie sehen und erleben dürfen, was geschaffen werden soll und wofür. Deshalb ist eine direkte Einbeziehung von Informations- und Bildungsarbeit in diese Naturschutzansätze erforderlich, um den eingeschlagenen Weg konfliktfrei und mit größtmöglicher Unterstützung der wirtschaftenden Menschen vor Ort weitergehen zu können. Hierfür wurden gerade an der Wurster Küste in den vergangenen Jahren viele positive Beispiele gelebt. Eine zukunftsfähige Lebensweise der Menschen in dieser Region wird immer mehr dadurch geprägt sein, inwieweit es gelingt, nachhaltige Formen des Lebens und Wirtschaftens umzusetzen.

Perspektivwechsel wie in diesem Bildband sind erforderlich, um die Dinge in Gänze zu betrachten. Die wunderbare Natur, die faszinierende Schönheit des Raumes wird oft erst bei Betrachtung aller Perspektiven erkannt. Möge dieses Buch dazu beitragen, dass immer mehr Menschen sich dem Erhalt unserer einzigartigen Natur am Wattenmeer und den Ästuaren von Elbe oder Weser verschreiben, dass sie mithelfen, diesen fantastischen Naturraum für nachfolgende Generationen zu bewahren.

Peter Südbeck
Leiter der Nationalpark- und Biosphärenreservatsverwaltung niedersächsisches Wattenmeer

THE WADDEN SEA

NATURAL SURROUNDINGS OF WORLDWIDE SIGNIFICANCE

People often need a change in perspective in order to experience and perceive new things. Martin Elsen's photographs offer us this changed perspective with completely new impressions and ways of viewing our immediate surroundings, through images of motifs that are unfamiliar to us or that we have not seen quite in this way.

The Wadden Sea is also in need of a change in perspective if one wishes to understand it. Most people only know the Wadden Sea from the dyke; the endless expanse at the Wurster Coast, brown-grey at low tide. The large tide-ways appear as lifelines. When one steps into the mudflats, accompanied by a National Park Mudflat tour guide, one learns of the smallest details; blow-lug sand-hills, bivalve breathing holes or the delicate scratch marks of sandhoppers, who draw filigree yet tiny patterns on the surface of the mud.
However, seen from the air, the Wadden Sea offers something completely different: the expanse assumes another dimension, as it is not monotone and homogenous but sprinkled with large or small, or thousands of the tiniest, tide-ways, which form their own pattern for the draining and irrigation of the mudflats, for their life elixir; the North Sea water. These patterns are only constant in a photograph. In nature, they change their appearance from day to day. In short time frames only minimally, calculated in terms of the human lifespan the tide-ways and mudflats, islands and salt marshes change significantly, often so that they are not recognisable.
The Wadden Sea at our coast – from the Netherlands to Denmark – is absolutely unique; there is no other such expansive, uninterrupted, young and dynamic landscape anywhere in the world. UNESCO gave it World Heritage status in 2009 as an indispensable part of our environment for the whole of humanity, as part of our responsibility on behalf of the whole of humankind. A great honour, and high recognition yet also a great challenge for those who are responsible for its protection.
Millions of sandhoppers, blow lugs and bivalves characterise the biology of the Wadden Sea, species that have the special ability to withstand the rigours of this environment; the tides and the changes in temperatures, salt content, currents and light intensity associated with them. They have developed strategies to survive nevertheless, which they do in very high numbers, as every tide and the inflows of water from the Elbe, Weser, Ems and Jade bring a constant supply of nutrition for these animals so that

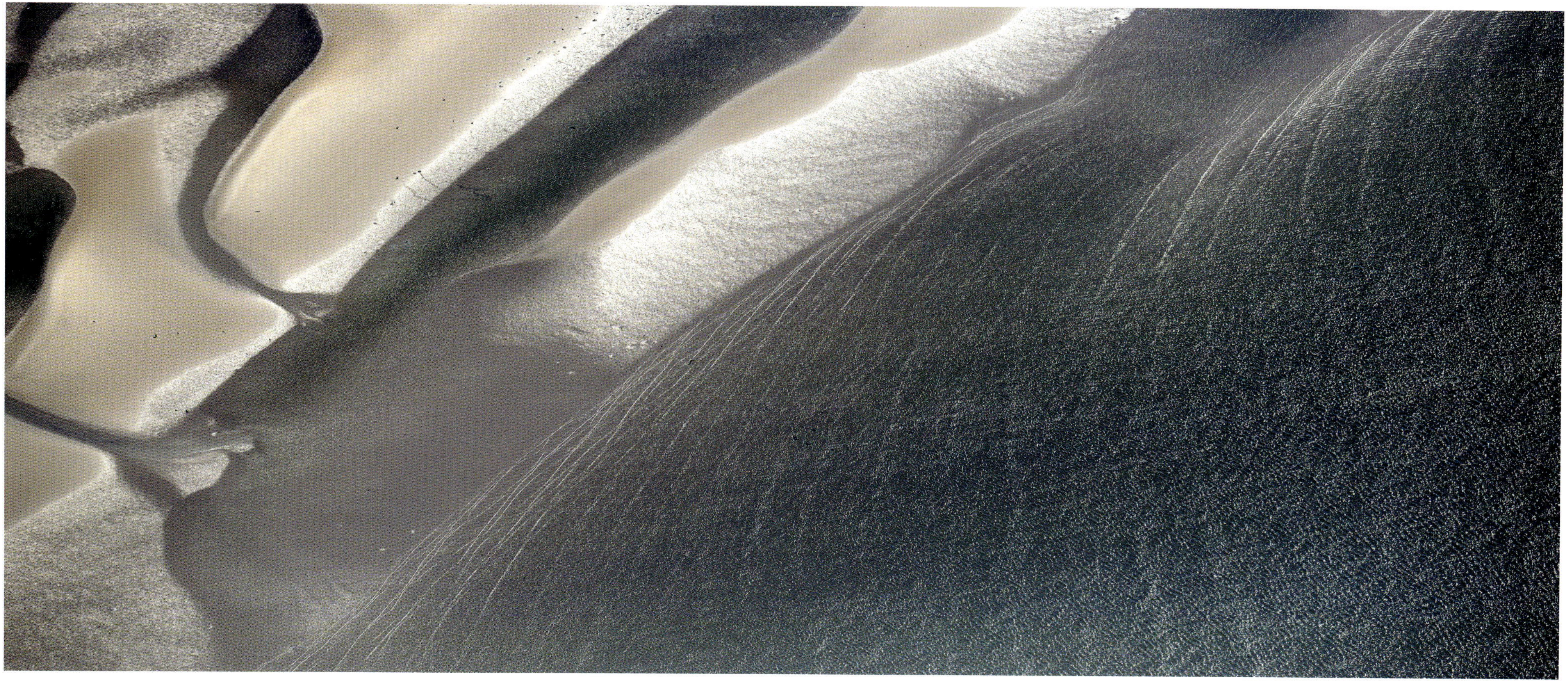

FASZINATION WATTENMEER
FASCINATING WADDEN SEA

extremely high population densities are achieved – a land of plenty! Thus, more than 100 000 sandhoppers have been counted on a square meter of watt. This is the basis for further links in the food chain of the Wadden Sea, especially migratory birds marine mammals such as seals.

This magnificent picture book, which and reveals this landscape from a unique perspective, is an invitation to the change in perception, which the Wadden Sea needs like no other habitat. People are fascinated by this unspoiled nature; every year hundreds of thousands visit the Wadden Sea, and the National Park buildings, millions of guests come to us because of these special natural surroundings and the vast majority of these people supports active and well-organised natural conservation in order to sustain these special features. ´The nature reserve at the Wadden Sea experiences extraordinary support today from the people who holiday here, and the people who live and work here, because they know that a livable environment is essential and necessary for successful community life.

Bringing man and nature together, in an area such as the Wadden Sea, or on the Lower Elbe, is a major prerequisite for people to live good lives and to secure the future for protecting nature. Martin Elsen's photographs make it especially clear how closely connected commerce and nature are in this area. Both "worlds" often encounter each other directly and unrestrainedly and the observer feels the tension between both sides. One side characterises economic prosperity, while the other represents a livable environment, which is of increasing importance for social cooperation and is essential for many new prospective residents in times of demographic change. In this respect, our space also stands for building bridges between the two seemingly opposite spheres of nature and the economy, and filling it with life. There are good examples of these bridges at our Wadden Sea coast; the container port Bremerhaven borders the Lower Saxony Wadden Sea National Park directly. With this reserve, the entire Wadden Sea off the coast of Lower Saxony was given protected status in 1986, which was essential for the region's receiving World Heritage status.

As part of the container port construction, alternative measures were implemented that have led the National Park to more Wadden Sea nature, former summer polders were re-cultivated and developed into valuable habitats for the Wadden Sea birds and plants. So besides the strong intervention in the Weser mudflats through the port construction, a significant contribution could also be made to the Wadden Sea itself. This is only possible when the people are convinced that such measures are meaningful, when they see and can experience what can be created and for what reason. Therefore, including information and education in these conservation approaches is required to continue on this path without conflict and with the greatest possible support from the local business people. Many positive examples of this were lived out at the Wurster coast in recent years. A sustainable lifestyle among the people in this region is influenced more and more by the extent to which it is possible to implement sustainable ways of living and economic activity.

Changes in perspective as those in this picture book are necessary in order to see things in their entirety. The wonderful nature, the amazing beauty of the space is often only recognised when all perspectives are considered. May this book be a factor in more and more people committing to sustaining our unique natural landscape at the Wadden Sea and the Elbe and Weser estuaries, and to preserving this wonderful environment for future generations.

Peter Südbeck
Director of the Nationalpark- und Biosphärenreservatsverwaltung niedersächsisches Wattenmeer (National Park and Biosphere Administration of the Lower Saxony Wadden Sea)

FLIGHTPLAN

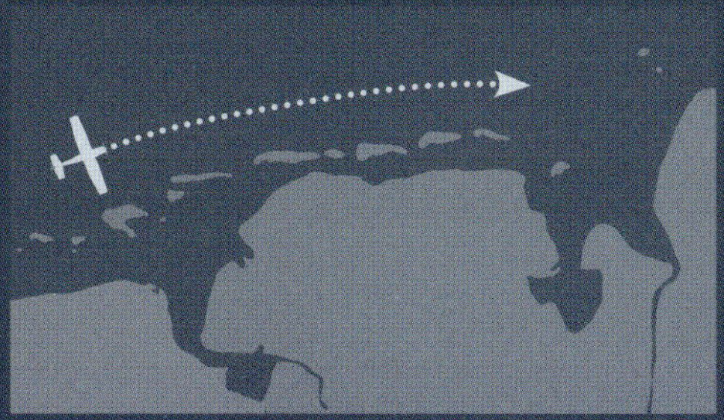

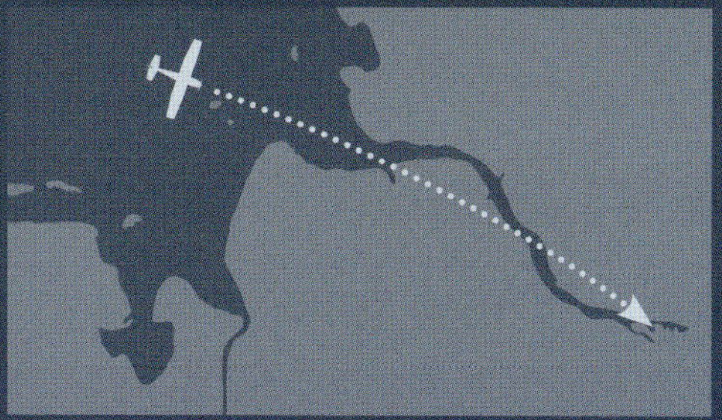

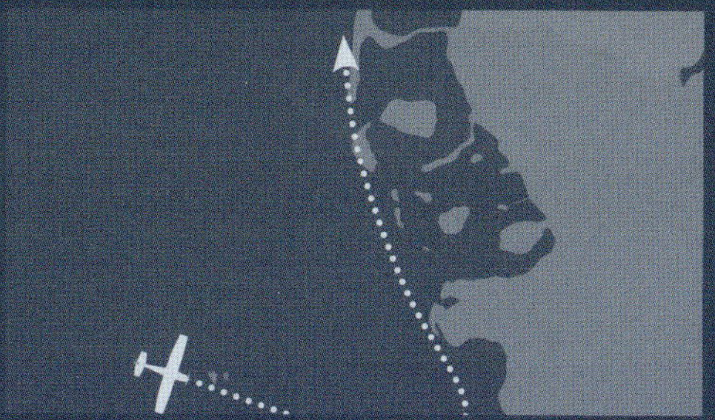

OSTFRIESISCHE KÜSTE

STRANDPROMENADE AUF BORKUM
BEACH PROMENADE ON THE ISLAND OF BORKUM

53° 38‘ 1.074“ N · 6° 44‘ 10.632“ E

KACHELOTPLATE, DIE INSELN JUIST, NORDERNEY UND DIE VOGELSCHUTZINSEL MEMMERT
KACHELOTPLATE, THE ISLANDS JUIST, NORDERNEY AND THE BIRD SANCTUARY ISLAND MEMMERT

SANDBANK DER KACHELOTPLATE,
IM HINTERGRUND VOGELSCHUTZINSEL MEMMERT
SANDBANK ON THE KACHELOTPLATE,
BIRD SANCTUARY ISLAND MEMMERT IN THE BACKGROUND

VOGELSCHUTZINSEL MEMMERT
BIRD SANCTUARY ISLAND MEMMERT

DIE SALZWIESEN AUF MEMMERT SIND EIN IDEALES BRUTGEBIET FÜR VÖGEL
THE SALT MARSHES ON MEMMERT ARE AN IDEAL BREEDING GROUND FOR BIRDS

OFFSHORE-WINDPARK VOR BORKUM
WINDPARK OFF THE SHORES OF BORKUM

BORKUMS WESTKÜSTE
BORKUM'S WEST COAST

BORKUM IST DIE WESTLICHSTE DER OSTFRIESISCHEN INSELN
BORKUM IS THE WESTERNMOST OF THE EAST FRIESIAN ISLANDS

BORKUMER STRAND-ANSICHT
BEACH VIEW OF BORKUM

NEUER LEUCHTTURM AUF DER INSEL BORKUM
NEW LIGHTHOUSE ON THE ISLAND OF BORKUM

BORKUMER HÄFEN
BORKUM HARBOURS

JUIST: DER HAMMERSEE IST DER EINZIGE SÜSSWASSERSEE DER OSTFRIESISCHEN INSELN
JUIST: LAKE HAMMERSEE IS THE ONLY FRESH WATER LAKE ON THE EAST FRIESIAN ISLANDS

HAFEN AUF JUIST MIT DEM NEUEN WAHRZEICHEN IN DER EINFAHRT
THE HARBOUR ON JUIST WITH ITS NEW LANDMARK AT THE ENTRANCE

JUIST-ANSICHTEN: FLUGHAFEN
VIEWS OF JUIST: AIRPORT

STRAND
BEACH

STRANDHOTEL UND KURHAUS
STRANDHOTEL AND KURHAUS (SPA)

FÄHRVERKEHR ZUR INSEL NORDERNEY
FERRY ON THE WAY TO NORDERNEY

CAFÉ IN DEN DÜNEN
CAFÉ IN THE DUNES

FÄHRE NACH NORDDEICH AUFS FESTLAND
FERRY TO NORDDEICH ON THE MAINLAND

NORDERNEY: DIE GANZE INSEL IM BLICK
NORDERNEY: AN OVERVIEW OF THE ENTIRE ISLAND

NORDERNEY: HAFEN MIT DER FÄHRE ZUM FESTLAND
NORDERNEY: HARBOUR INCLUDING THE FERRY TO THE MAINLAND

DAS KURGEBIET VON NORDERNEY
THE SPA AREA OF NORDERNEY

SALZWIESEN VON NORDERNEY
SALT MARSHES ON NORDERNEY

DER NORDERNEYER YACHTHAFEN
THE NORDERNEY MARINA

ANSICHTEN VON NORDERNEY: INSEL ZWISCHEN MEER UND WATT
VIEWS OF NORDERNEY: ISLAND BETWEEN SEA AND MUDFLATS

DIE DÜNENLANDSCHAFT
DUNE LANDSCAPE

DIE SALZWIESEN
THE SALT MARSHES

DIE FÄHRE NACH NORDDEICH
THE FERRY TO NORDDEICH

DIE „MILCHBAR“ AM MEER
THE “MILCHBAR” AT THE BEACH

NESSMERSIEL
NESSMERSIEL

BALTRUM (IM HINTERGRUND DIE INSEL LANGEOOG)
BALTRUM (WITH THE ISLAND OF LANGEOOG IN THE BACKGROUND)

DIE WESTKÜSTE VON BALTRUM
THE WEST COAST OF BALTRUM

FERIENSIEDLUNG AUF BALTRUM
HOLIDAY VILLAGE ON BALTRUM

BALTRUM MIT FÄHRE UND YACHTHAFEN
BALTRUM WITH FERRY AND MARINA

DORNUMERSIEL LIEGT DIREKT AN DER KÜSTE
DORNUMERSIEL IS RIGHT ON THE COAST

DER YACHTHAFEN IN DORNUMERSIEL
THE MARINA ON DORNUMERSIEL

DIE FÄHRE VON DORNUMERSIEL NACH LANGEOOG
THE FERRY FROM DORNUMERSIEL TO LANGEOOG

LANGEOOGS SCHÖNE DÜNENLANDSCHAFT
LANGEOOG'S BEAUTIFUL DUNE LANDSCAPE

LANGEOOG – DIE INSEL SIEHT AUS WIE EIN „L" IN DER NORDSEE
LANGEOOG – THE ISLAND LOOKS LIKE AN 'L' IN THE NORTH SEA

NOCH EINMAL LANGEOOGS DÜNEN
MORE OF LANGEOOG'S DUNES

DER LANGEOOGER HAFEN
THE LANGEOOG HARBOUR

LANGEOOGS ÜPPIGER STRAND
LANGEOOG'S LUXURIANT BEACH

LANGEOOGER ANSICHTEN: DIE SÜDERDÜNEN
VIEWS OF LANGEOOG: THE SOUTHERN DUNES

EIN GROSSES ZELTLAGER AUF LANGEOOG
A LARGE TENT CAMP ON LANGEOOG

EIN VERSORGER DER DEUTSCHEN MARINE UND
EINE FREGATTE DER BELGISCHEN MARINE (OBEN)
A GERMAN MARINE WORK BOAT AND A BELGIAN MARINE FRIGATE

BENSERSIEL: NORDSEEHEILBAD AN DER OSTFRIESISCHEN KÜSTE
BENSERSIEL: NORTH SEA SPA TOWN ON THE EAST FRIESIAN COAST

NEUHARLINGERSIEL HAT EINEN EIGENEN STRAND UND HAFEN
NEUHARLINGERSIEL HAS ITS OWN BEACH AND HARBOUR

SPIEKEROOG MIT SANDBANK
SPIEKEROOG WITH SANDBANK

SALZWIESEN AUF DER INSEL SPIEKEROOG
SALT MARSHES ON THE ISLAND OF SPIEKEROOG

OSTKÜSTE VON SPIEKEROOG
EAST COAST OF SPIEKEROOG

SPIEKEROOGER HAFEN
SPIEKEROOG HARBOUR

ANSICHTEN VON SPIEKEROOG
VIEWS OF SPIEKEROOG

INSELSIEDLUNG
ISLAND RESIDENTIAL AREA

SCHULZENTRUM
SCHOOL COMPLEX

WANGEROOGE MIT SPIEKEROOG UND LANGEOOG (IM HINTERGRUND)
WANGEROOGE WITH SPIEKEROOG AND LANGEOOG (IN THE BACKGROUND)

WANGEROOGER WESTANSICHT
WESTERN VIEW OF WANGEROOGE

OSTANSICHT
EASTERN VIEW

INSELZENTRUM
ISLAND CENTRE

MARKANTE JUGENDHERBERGE
DISTINCTIVE YOUTH HOSTEL

OSTSPITZE AUF WANGEROOGE – EIN BELIEBTER ANKERPLATZ UNTER SEGLERN
EASTERN TIP OF WANGEROOGE – A WELL-LOVED ANCHORING BERTH AMONG SAILING ENTHUSIASTS

ALTER LEUCHTTURM VON WANGEROOGE
THE OLD LIGHTHOUSE OF WANGEROOGE

WANGEROOGER BUHNEN AUF DER WESTSEITE
SPUR DYKES ON THE WEST COAST OF WANGEROOGE

MORGENGYMNASTIK AM WANGEROOGER STRAND
MORNING GYMNASTICS ON THE BEACH ON WANGEROOGE

MINSENER OOG AN DER WESERMÜNDUNG
MIT JADE WESER PORT WILHELMSHAVEN
MINSENER OOG ON THE WESER ESTUARY
INCLUDING THE JADE WESER PORT OF
WILHELMSHAVEN

MINSENER OOG – VIEL SAND, WENIG GRÜN
MINSENER OOG – LOTS OF SAND, LITTLE VEGETATION

WESERMÜNDUNG
WESER ESTUARY

JADEBUSEN UND WESER

WILHELMSHAVEN: WOHNEN AM WASSER
WILHELMSHAVEN: LIVING ON THE COAST

DEUTSCHES MARINE-MUSEUM IN WILHELMSHAVEN
GERMAN MARINE MUSEUM IN WILHELMSHAVEN

DIE KAISER-WILHELM-BRÜCKE IN WILHELMSHAVEN
THE KAISER WILHELM BRIDGE IN WILHELMSHAVEN

JADE WESER PORT
JADE WESER PORT

BLICK AUF WILHELMSHAVEN
VIEW OF WILHELMSHAVEN

JADE WESER PORT, NOCH ALS BAUSTELLE
JADE WESER PORT DURING CONSTRUCTION

CONTAINER-KRÄNE IM JADE WESER PORT
CONTAINER CRANES AT THE JADE WESER PORT

JADE WESER PORT NACH DER FERTIGSTELLUNG
JADE WESER PORT FOLLOWING COMPLETION

DER KLEINE ORT BURHAVE AN DER WESERMÜNDUNG
BURHAVE ON THE WESER ESTUARY

HAFENSTADT NORDENHAM AN DER WESER
THE PORT TOWN OF NORDENHAM ON THE WESER

DAS AIRBUSWERK IN NORDENHAM
THE AIRBUS PLANT IN NORDENHAM

NORDENHAM LIEGT DIREKT AN DER WESER
NORDENHAM IS SITUATED DIRECTLY ON THE BANKS OF THE WESER

NORDENHAM IST EINE BEDEUTENDE HAFENSTADT IN NIEDERSACHSEN
NORDENHAM IS A SIGNIFICANT PORT TOWN IN LOWER SAXONY

NORDENHAMER ANSICHTEN:
FIRMA PENSHORN & SÖHNE
VIEWS OF NORDENHAM:
THE COMPANY PENSHORN UND SOEHNE

TANKLAGER IM HAFEN
TANK FARM IN THE HARBOUR

WESERFÄHRE AUF DEM WEG
NACH BREMERHAVEN-BLEXEN
WESER FERRY ON THE WAY
TO BREMERHAVEN-BLEXEN

DER MARKTPLATZ IM ZENTRUM
THE MARKETPLACE IN THE CENTRE

DER GATETEICH
THE GATETEICH (GATE POND)

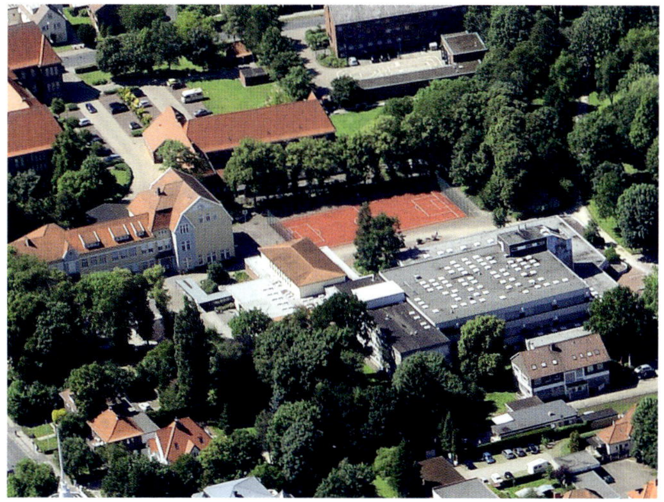

DIE STADTBÜCHEREI
THE CITY LIBRARY

WALLENIUS WILHELMSEN

BREMERHAVEN MIT SEINEM HAFENGELÄNDE
BREMERHAVEN WITH ITS HARBOUR AREA

BREMERHAVEN: INNENSTADT MIT KLIMAHAUS UND DEM HOTEL ATLANTIC
BREMERHAVEN: INNER CITY WITH “KLIMAHAUS” AND THE HOTEL ATLANTIC

DER ZOO IN BREMERHAVEN
THE ZOO IN BREMERHAVEN

BREMERHAVEN IN DER GESAMTANSICHT VON OBEN
AN AERIAL VIEW OF THE ENTIRE AREA OF BREMERHAVEN

DER FISCHEREIHAFEN VON BREMERHAVEN
THE FISHING PORT AT BREMERHAVEN

BREMERHAVENER ANSICHTEN: CONTAINERUMSCHLAG
VIEWS OF BREMERHAVEN: CONTAINER HANDLING

SCHIFF IM TROCKENDOCK
SHIP IN DRY DOCK

AUTOTRANSPORTER VON WALLENIUS WILHELMSEN
AUTO TRANSPORTERS OWEND BY WALLENIUS WILHELMSEN

NOCH EINMAL TROCKENDOCKS
DRY DOCKS ONCE MORE

DER YACHTHAFEN AN DER WESER
THE MARINA ON THE WESER

CONTAINER-TERMINAL
CONTAINER TERMINAL

CONTAINERABFERTIGUNG IN BREMERHAVEN
CONTAINER HANDLING IN BREMERHAVEN

OFFSHORE VERLADUNG IM ÜBERSEEHAFEN
OFFSHORE LOADING IN THE OVERSEAS PORT

SCHIFF IM TROCKENDOCK IM ÜBERSEEHAFEN
SHIP IN DRY DOCK IN THE OVERSEAS PORT

UMSCHLAGPLATZ FÜR AUTOS: VERLADUNG IM ÜBERSEEHAFEN
AUTOMOBILE HANDLING AREA: LOADING AT OVERSEAS PORT

FIRMA J.MÜLLER, HAFENDIENSTLEISTER IN BRAKE
THE COMPANY J. MUELLER, PORT SERVICES PROVIDER IN BRAKE

SIELBAUWERK IM ORTSTEIL KÄSEBURG DER STADT BRAKE
SLUICE STRUCTURES IN THE BRAKE DISTRICT OF KAESEBURG

HAMMELWARDEN, LINKS DER ALTE WASSERTURM
HAMMELWARDEN WITH THE OLD WATER TOWER TO THE LEFT

WINDKRAFTANLAGEN AUF HALDE
STOCKED WIND TURBINES

BINNENHAFEN IN BRAKE
INLAND PORT IN BRAKE

BREMER ALTSTADT
BREMEN'S OLD TOWN

BREMER ALTSTADT, WESER
BREMEN'S OLD TOWN, WESER

BREMER ALTSTADT, WILHELM-KAISEN-BRÜCKE
BREMEN'S OLD TOWN, WILHELM KAISEN BRIDGE

RATHAUS, RATHAUSPLATZ
TOWN HALL, TOWN HALL SQUARE

BREMER DOM
BREMEN CATHEDRAL

WESER, „KLEINE WESER“, TEERHOFINSEL
WESER, “KLEINE WESER”, TEERHOFINSEL

GASTROSCHIFF ADMIRAL NELSON · KIRCHE ST. MARTINI
RESTAURANT SHIP ADMIRAL NELSON · ST. MARTINI CHURCH

SHOPPING-CENTER WATERFRONT BREMEN
WATERFRONT SHOPPING CENTRE BREMEN

DORINT PARK HOTEL BREMEN
DORINT PARK HOTEL BREMEN

BREMER SCHNOOR
BREMER SCHNOOR

BREMEN HAUPTBAHNHOF
BREMEN MAIN TRAIN STATION

ST.-MARTINI-KIRCHE · DRACHENBOOTRENNEN AUF DER WESER
ST. MARTINI CHURCH · DRAGON BOAT RACE ON THE WESER

BREMEN NEUSTADT
BREMEN NEUSTADT

BREMER WESERSTADION
THE WESER STADIUM BREMEN

BREMEN VEGESACK
BREMEN VEGESACK

SWB-HEIZKRAFTWERK HASTEDT
SWB THERMAL POWER STATION, HASTEDT

FLUGZEUG DER TURKISH AIRLINES IM LANDEANFLUG AUF BREMEN
TURKISH AIRLINES PLANE ON APPROACH TO BREMEN

BECK'S BIERKISTEN IN BREMEN NEUSTADT
BECK'S BEER CRATES IN BREMEN NEUSTADT

BREMER VERKEHRSFLUGHAFEN
AIRPORT BREMEN

BREMER MESSE, RECHTS ARENA VON BREMEN
BREMEN'S CONFERENCE CENTRE, WITH THE BREMEN ARENA ON THE RIGHT

BREMER STRASSENBAHN DEPOT
BREMEN'S TRAM DEPOT

Pelorus

DIE AZZAM IST MIT EINER LÄNGE VON 180 METERN DIE LÄNGSTE PRIVATE YACHT DER WELT.
EIGNER IST DER PRÄSIDENT DER VEREINIGTEN ARABISCHEN EMIRATE
THE AZZAM, WITH ITS 180 METERS, IS THE LONGEST PRIVATE YACHT IN THE WORLD.
IT IS OWNED BY THE PRESIDENT OF THE UNITED ARAB EMIRATES

PELORUS, 115 METER LANG, BIS 2012 DIE YACHT VON ROMAN ABRAMOWITSCH
PELORUS, 115 METERS LONG, BELONGED TO ROMAN ABRAMOWITSCH UNTIL 2012

DER LEUCHTTURM „HOHE WEG“ IST DER
ÄLTESTE LEUCHTTURM IN DER AUSSENWESER
THE LIGHTHOUSE “HOHE WEG” IS THE OLDEST
LIGHTHOUSE ON THE OUTER WESER

WINDRAD VOR DEM JADE WESER PORT
WIND TURBINE AT THE JADE WESER PORT

SEGLER IM JADEBUSEN
SAILERS IN THE JADEBUSEN

EIN WRACK IN DER WESERMÜNDUNG
A WRECK IN THE WESER ESTUARY

LEUCHTTURM „MELLUMPLATE" IN DER DEUTSCHEN BUCHT VOR WILHELMSHAVEN
THE LIGHTHOUSE MELLUMPLATE IN THE GERMAN BIGHT OFF THE COAST OF WILHELMSHAVEN

„ALEXANDER VON HUMBOLDT" UNTER SEGELN
THE "ALEXANDER VON HUMBOLDT" UNDER SAIL

FASZINATION WATTENMEER
FASCINATING WADDEN SEA

DAS ALTE-LAND – EUROPAS GRÖSSTES GESCHLOSSENES OBSTANBAUGEBIET
THE “ALTE LAND” – EUROPE’S LARGEST INDIVIDUAL FRUIT GROWING AREA

DEUTSCHE BUCHT UND ELBE

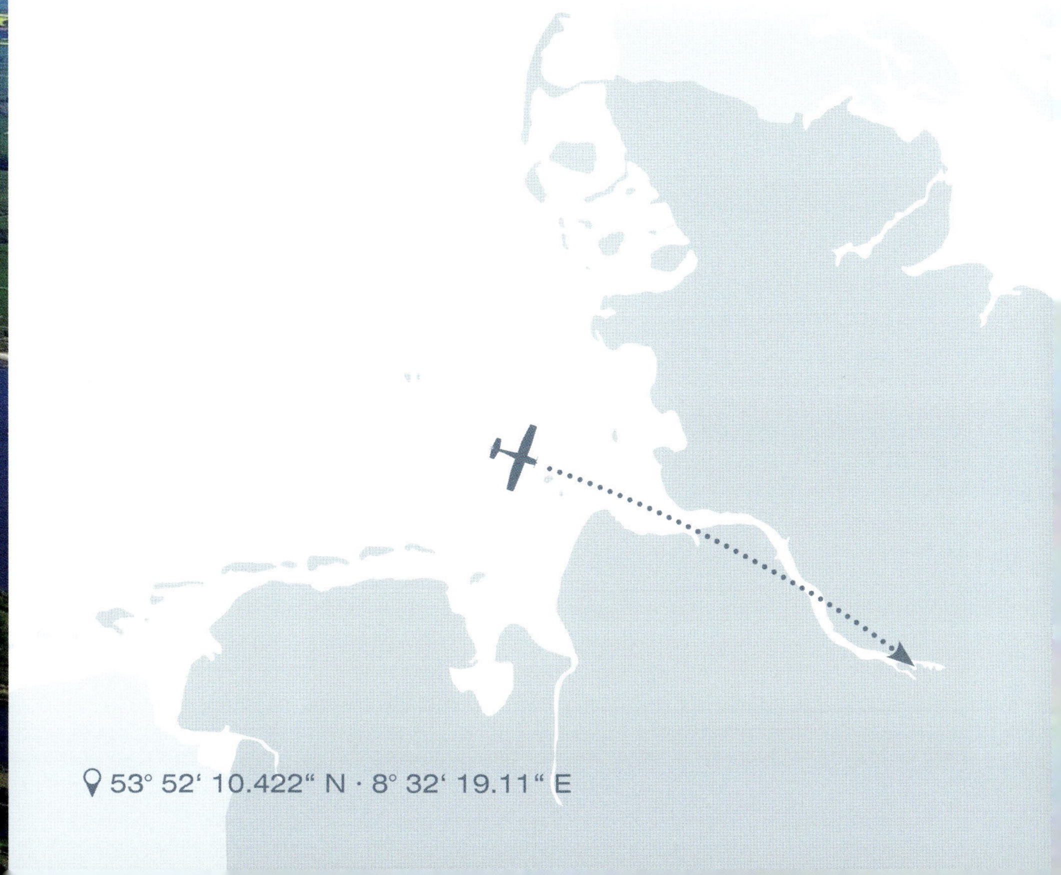

DIE INSEL NEUWERK LIEGT MITTEN IM WATT VOR CUXHAVEN
THE ISLAND NEUWERK IS IN THE MIDDLE OF THE WADDEN SEA OFF THE COAST OF CUXHAVEN

WATTENMEER VOR CUXHAVEN
WADDEN SEA AT CUXHAVEN COAST

WATTENMEER VOR DER WESERMÜNDUNG
WADDEN SEA AT THE WESER ESTUARY

WATTENMEER VOR DER EIDER
WADDEN SEA AT THE EIDER

WATTENMEER IN DER DEUTSCHEN BUCHT
WADDEN SEA IN THE GERMAN BIGHT

WATTENMEER VOR SAHLENBURG
WADDEN SEA AT THE SAHLENBURG COAST

WATTENMEER VOR CUXHAVEN
WADDEN SEA AT CUXHAVEN COAST

DIE VOGELSCHUTZINSELN SCHARHÖRN UND NIGEHÖRN
THE BIRD SANCTUARY ISLANDS SCHARHOERN AND NIGEHOERN

BLICK AUF NEUWERK
VIEW OF NEUWERK

MS FLIPPER FÄHRT VON NEUWERK NACH CUXHAVEN
TRIP WITH MS FLIPPER FROM NEUWERK TO CUXHAVEN

NEUWERK, ÄLTESTER DEUTSCHER LEUCHTTURM AUS DEM JAHR 1310
NEUWERK, OLDEST GERMAN LIGHTHOUSE FROM THE YEAR 1310

URLAUBERZENTRUM SAHLENBURG BEI CUXHAVEN
HOLIDAY CENTRE SAHLENBURG NEAR CUXHAVEN

CUXHAVENS WAHRZEICHEN, DIE KUGELBAKE
CUXHAVEN'S LANDMARK THE "KUGELBAKE"

DAS CUXHAVENER KURGEBIET
THE CUXHAVEN SPA AREA

OTTERNDORF: FERIENANLAGE AN DER ELBE
OTTERNDORF: HOLIDAY RESORT ON THE ELBE

DIE ALTSTADT VON OTTERNDORF
OTTERNDORF'S OLD TOWN

DAS DORF NEUHAUS AN DER OSTEMÜNDUNG
THE VILLAGE OF NEUHAUS ON THE OSTE ESTUARY

DAS OSTESPERRWERK (IM HINTERGRUND DIE WASSERSKIANLAGE NEUHAUS)
THE OSTE BARRAGE (THE NEUHAUS WATER SKIING FACILITY CAN BE SEEN IN THE BACKGROUND)

DER HEMMOORER KREIDESEE –
EIN ELDORADO FÜR TAUCHER AUS GANZ DEUTSCHLAND
THE HEMMOOR KREIDESEE – AN ELDORADO FOR DIVERS ALL OVER GERMANY

NOCH EINMAL KREIDESEE: FLUGZEUG UNTER WASSER
THE KREIDESEE: AIRPLANE UNDER WATER

DAS NATURKUNDEMUSEUM NATUREUM AN DER OSTE
THE NATURAL HISTORY MUSEUM ON THE BANKS OF THE OSTE

DENKMALGESCHÜTZTE SCHWEBEFÄHRE IN OSTEN
PROTECTED SUSPENSION FERRY IN OSTEN

DIE OSTE MIT IHRER IDYLLISCHEN FLUSSLANDSCHAFT
THE OSTE AND ITS IDYLLIC RIVER LANDSCAPE

DIE SCHWEBEFÄHRE ÜBER DIE OSTE
THE SUSPENSION FERRY OVER THE OSTE

DER NORD-OSTSEE-KANAL UND DIE SCHLEUSEN IN BRUNSBÜTTEL
THE KIEL CANAL AND SLUICES IN BRUNSBUETTEL

CONTAINERSCHIFF AUF DEM NORD-OSTSEE-KANAL
MIT DER HOCHBRÜCKE VOR BRUNSBÜTTEL
CONTAINER SHIP ON THE KIEL CANAL
WITH THE HIGH BRIDGE NEAR BRUNSBUETTEL

NORD-OSTSEE-KANAL – SCHLEUSEN ALS ÜBERGANG IN DIE ELBMÜNDUNG
KIEL CANAL SLUICES AS A JUNCTION TO THE ELBE ESTUARY

DER NORD-OSTSEE-KANAL
THE KIEL CANAL

DER BRUNSBÜTTEL PORT
THE BRUNSBUETTEL PORT

SCHIFFSVERKEHR AUF DEM GROSSEN KANAL
SHIPPING TRAFFIC ON THE LARGE CANAL

GEGENVERKEHR AUF DEM KANAL
BIDIRECTIONAL TRAFFIC ON THE CANAL

DAS KRAFTWERK IN BRUNSBÜTTEL
THE POWER STATION IN BRUNSBUETTEL

GLÜCKSTADT: INNENSTADT MIT MARKTPLATZ
GLUECKSTADT: INNER CITY WITH MARKET PLACE

WISCHHAFEN MIT DER FÄHRVERBINDUNG VON GLÜCKSTADT
WISCHHAFEN WITH THE FERRY CONNECTION TO GLUECKSTADT

DIE AUTOFÄHRE BEI DER ABFAHRT AUS GLÜCKSTADT
THE CAR FERRY LEAVING GLUECKSTADT

FISCHERBOOT IN DER ELBMÜNDUNG
FISHING BOAT IN THE ELBE ESTUARY

DER FÄHRANLEGER IN GLÜCKSTADT
THE FERRY PORT IN GLUECKSTADT

DIE ELBMARSCH IN SÜDKEHDINGEN
THE ELBE MARSHES IN SUEDKEHDINGEN

ELBINSEL KRAUTSAND AM RUTHENSTROM MIT DEM SPERRWERK
ELBE ISLAND KRAUTSAND AT THE "RUTHENSTROM" WITH THE BARRAGE

KRAUTSAND MIT SEINEM STRAND UND DEM SCHIFFSANLEGER
KRAUTSAND WITH ITS BEACH AND THE JETTY

DORNBUSCH – ORTSCHAFT AN DER UNTERELBE
DORNBUSCH – VILLAGE ON THE LOWER ELBE

DROCHTERSEN LIEGT NAHE DER ELBE
DROCHTERSEN IS LOCATED CLOSE TO THE ELBE

DROCHTERSER RATHAUS
DROCHTERSEN TOWN HALL

DROCHTERSER ELBMARSCHEN-SCHULE
DROCHTERSEN'S ELBMARSCHEN SCHOOL

BOOTSWERFT HATECKE AUF KRAUTSAND
SHIPYARD HATECKE ON KRAUTSAND

DIE KIRCHE VON ASSEL
THE CHURCH IN ASSEL

GESAMTBLICK AUF ASSEL
ENTIRE OVERVIEW OF ASSEL

ELBNEBENARM BEI DROCHTERSEN
ELBE TRIBUTARY NEAR DROCHTERSEN

FORT GRAUERORT MIT STILLGELEGTEM ANLEGER BEI STADE
GRAUERORT FORT WITH DISUSED JETTY NEAR STADE

WEWELSFLETH: PETERS-WERFT AN DER STÖR
WEWELSFLETH: PETERS-WERFT ON THE STOER

DIE OSTEMÜNDUNG BEI BALJE
THE OSTE ESTUARY NEAR BALJE

DIE ELBINSEL SCHWARZTONNENSAND
THE ELBE ISLAND SCHWARZTONNENSAND

DIE ELBINSEL LÜHESAND
THE ELBE ISLAND LUEHESAND

DIE ELBINSEL PAGENSAND
THE ELBE ISLAND PAGENSAND

STADERSAND: HIER MÜNDET DIE SCHWINGE IN DIE ELBE
STADERSAND: HERE IS WHERE THE SCHWINGE MERGES WITH THE ELBE

ZUSAMMENGEWACHSENE ELBINSELN HANSKALBSAND, NESSSAND UND SCHWEINESAND
THE AGGLOMERATED ELBE PENINSULAS HANSKALBSAND, NESSSAND AND SCHWEINESAND

SEEHAFEN STADE
STADE SEA PORT

DOW-WERK STADE
DOW PLANT AT STADE

ALUMINIUMOXID-WERK AOS IM INDUSTRIEGEBIET VON STADE-BÜTZFLETH
ALUMINIUM OXIDE PLANT AOS IN THE INDUSTRIAL PARK STADE-BUETZFLETH

SEEHAFEN STADE: HAFEN-SCHLEPPER DER FIRMA ELBCLEARING
STADE SEA PORT: THE COMPANY ELBCLEARING'S HARBOUR TUG-BOAT

SEEHAFEN STADE: VERLADUNG AM DOW-ANLEGER
STADE SEA PORT: LOADING AT DOW JETTY

STADER SEEHAFEN: VERLADUNG VON SCHÜTTGÜTERN AM BUSS-ANLEGER
STADE SEA PORT: LOADING OF BULK GOODS AT THE BUSS JETTY

DAS BAUXIT-LAGER VON AOS
AOS BAUXITE STOCK

DIE ROTSCHLAMMDEPONIE VON AOS IM BÜTZFLETHER MOOR
AOS RED MUD LANDFILL

ABGESCHALTETES STADER ATOMKRAFTWERK IM RÜCKBAU
STADE'S DECOMMISSIONED ATOMIC ENERGY PLANT IN THE PROCESS OF DEMOLITION

STADE: ALTSTADT MIT DER KIRCHE ST. COSMAE ET DAMIANI
STADE: OLD TOWN WITH THE CHURCH OF ST. COSMAE ET DAMIANI

HANSESTADT STADE MIT IHRER HISTORISCHEN ALTSTADT
THE HANSEATIC CITY OF STADE WITH ITS HISTORIC OLD TOWN

STADER ANSICHTEN: HAFENCITY
VIEW OF STADE: HARBOUR CITY

STADEUM – KULTUR- UND TAGUNGSZENTRUM
STADEUM – CULTURE AND CONFERENCE CENTRE

ELBE KLINIKEN
ELBE CLINICS

ST.-WILHADI-KIRCHE
ST WILHADI CHURCH

STADTHAFEN MIT DEM MUSEUMSSCHIFF GREUNDIEK
CITY PORT WITH THE MUSEUM SHIP GREUNDIEK

DER ALTE HANSEHAFEN AM FISCHMARKT
MIT DEM SCHWEDENSPEICHER
THE OLD HANSA PORT AT THE FISCHMARKT
WITH THE SCHWEDENSPEICHER (SWEDISH SPIRE)

KLINIK DR. HANCKEN (GELBES GEBÄUDE)
CLINIC DR. HANCKEN (YELLOW BUILDING)

STADE: IM SCHWINGETAL MÄANDERT DIE SCHWINGE
STADE: THE SCHWINGE MEANDERS THROUGH THE SCHWINGE VALLEY

AIRBUSWERK IN STADE
AIRBUS PLANT IN STADE

WEDEL – DER GRÖSSTE YACHTHAFEN AN DER ELBE
WEDEL – THE LARGEST MARINA ON THE ELBE

HANSESTADT BUXTEHUDE MIT IHREM ALTSTADTKERN
THE HANSEATIC CITY OF BUXTEHUDE WITH THE OLD TOWN CENTRE

RALLYCROSS-RENNSTRECKE ESTERING
RALLYCROSS CIRCUIT ESTERING

BUXTEHUDER ANSICHTEN: ST.-PETRI-KIRCHE
VIEWS OF BUXTEHUDE: ST. PETRI CHURCH

DAS STADTHAUS
THE TOWN HALL

DIE HOCHSCHULE 21
THE HOCHSCHULE 21 COLLEGE

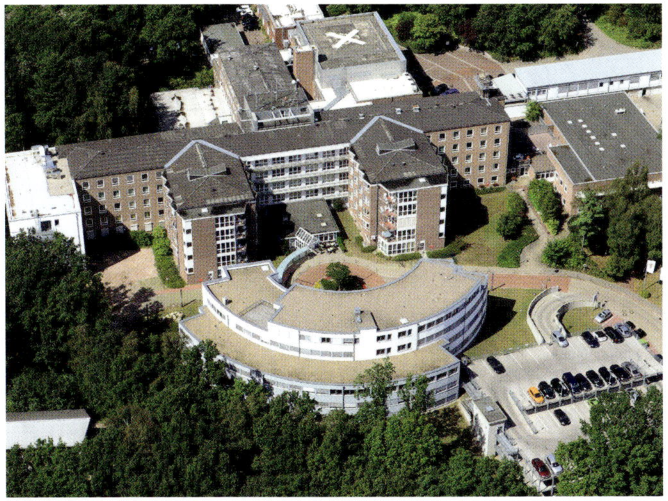

DIE ELBE KLINIKEN
THE ELBE CLINICS

DIE UNILEVER PRODUKTIONSANLAGEN
THE UNILEVER MANUFACTURING PLANTS

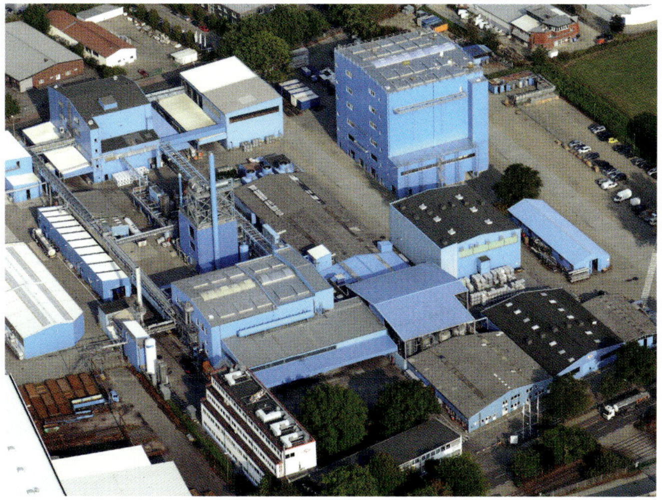

DIE SYNTHOPOL CHEMIEANLAGEN
THE SYNTHOPOL CHEMICAL PLANTS

DAS OBSTANBAUGEBIET „ALTES LAND“
THE FRUIT GROWING REGION “ALTES LAND”

TWIELENFLETH FERIENDORF (IM HINTERGRUND ELBINSEL LÜHESAND)
TWIELENFLETH HOLIDAY VILLAGE (THE ELBE ISLAND LUEHESAND CAN BE SEEN IN THE BACKGROUND)

GRÜNENDEICH UND STEINKIRCHEN IM „ALTEN LAND“
GRUENENDEICH AND STEINKIRCHEN IN THE “ALTES LAND”

STEINKIRCHEN MIT DER BEKANNTEN HOGENDIEKBRÜCKE
STEINKIRCHEN WITH THE WELL-KNOWN HOGENDIEK BRIDGE

DER ELBENEBENFLUSS LÜHE IM „ALTEN LAND“
THE ELBE TRIBUTARY LUEHE IN THE “ALTES LAND”

EUROPAS HÖCHSTE STROMMASTEN
STEHEN AUF LÜHESAND
EUROPE'S HIGHEST POWER PYLONS CAN
BE FOUND ON LUEHESAND

DIE HOGENDIEKBRÜCKE
IN STEINKIRCHEN
THE HOGENDIEK BRIDGE
IN STEINKIRCHEN

FLUSS AUF UMWEGEN:
DIE LÜHE MACHT EINEN GROSSEN BOGEN
MEANDERING RIVER:
THE LUEHE FORMS A LARGE CURVE

DER GRÜNENDEICHER LEUCHTTURM
THE GRUENENDEICH LIGHTHOUSE

DER LÜHE-ANLEGER AN DER ELBE
THE LUEHE JETTY ON THE ELBE

DIE KIRCHE IN JORK
THE CHURCH IN JORK

APFELBÄUME BEI JORK VOR DEN TOREN HAMBURGS
APPLE TREES NEAR JORK ON HAMBURG'S DOORSTEP

KÜSTENWACHE

UNIFEEDER
COSCO

KATAMARAN DER LINIE HAMBURG – HELGOLAND
KATAMARAN FROM THE HAMBURG – HELGOLAND LINE

KÜSTENWACHE IN DER ELBMÜNDUNG
COAST GUARD IN THE ELBE ESTUARY

SAUGBAGGER IN DER ELBE
SUCTION DREDGER ON THE ELBE

CONTAINERSCHIFF IN DER ELBE
CONTAINER SHIP ON THE ELBE

AIDA-KREUZFAHRTSCHIFF IN DER ELBE
AIDA CRUISE SHIP ON THE ELBE

KRABBENKUTTER IN DER ELBMÜNDUNG
SHRIMP VESSEL IN THE ELBE ESTUARY

SCHIFFE AUF DER ELBE: CONTAINERSCHIFF, ZWEI TANKER
SHIPS ON THE ELBE: CONTAINER SHIP, TWO TANKERS

CONTAINERSCHIFF JORK
CONTAINER SHIP JORK

SCHWERGUTFRACHER
HEAVY GOODS FREIGHTER

CHEMIEKALIEN-TANKER MIT LOTSENBOOT
CHEMICAL TANKER WITH PILOT BOAT

HAMBURG MIT LANDUNGSBRÜCKEN UND BINNENALSTER (IM HINTERGRUND)
HAMBURG WITH LANDUNGSBRUECKEN AND INNER ALSTER LAKE (IN THE BACKGROUND)

NEUENFELDE MIT DER SIETAS-WERFT
NEUENFELDE WITH THE SIETAS SHIPYARD

HANÖFERSAND MIT DEM JUGENDGEFÄNGNIS
HANOEFERSAND WITH THE JUVENILE PRISON

ELBINSEL HANSKALBSAND (IM HINTERGRUND WEDEL)
ELBE ISLAND HANSKALBSAND (WEDEL IN THE BACKGROUND)

FINKENWERDER: AIRBUSWERK MIT LANDEBAHN
FINKENWERDER: AIRBUS PLANT WITH RUNWAY

QATAR
القطرية

BELUGA AIRBUS
4

Lufthansa

DIE BELUGA TRANSPORTIERT TEILE VON FINKENWERDER NACH TOULOUSE
THE BELUGA TRANSPORTS PARTS FROM FINKENWERDER TO TOULOUSE

AIRBUS-IMPRESSIONEN AUS FINKENWERDER:
AIRBUS A380 FÜR KATAR
AIRBUS IMPRESSIONS FROM FINKENWERDER:
AIRBUS A380 FOR QATAR

DREI AIRBUS A380 AUF
DEM ROLLHALT
THREE A380S ON HOLDING POINTS

BELUGA – TRANSPORTMASCHINE
VON AIRBUS
AIRBUS BELUGA TRANSPORT PLANE

WERKSEINGANG VON AIRBUS
AIRBUS PLANT ENTRANCE

A380 BEIM TRIEBWERKSCHECK
A380 UNDERGOING ENGINE CHECKS

DER ERSTE A380 FÜR DIE LUFTHANSA
THE FIRST A380 FOR LUFTHANSA

CONTAINERLAGER IM HAFEN
CONTAINER STORAGE IN THE HARBOUR

HAMBURGER HAFEN MIT DIVERSEN TERMINALS
HAMBURG HARBOUR WITH VARIOUS TERMINALS

AUF DER KÖHLBRANDBRÜCKE DURCH DEN HAFEN
THROUGH THE HARBOUR VIA THE KOEHLBRAND BRIDGE

HAMBURGER HAFENIMPRESSIONEN: CONTAINERHÄFEN
IMPRESSIONS OF HAMBURG HARBOUR: CONTAINER PORTS

HAMBURGS NEUE HAFENCITY
MIT DER ELBPHILHARMONIE
HAMBURG'S NEW "HAFENCITY"
WITH THE ELBPHILHARMONIE

LANDUNGSBRÜCKEN MIT DEM ALTEN ELBTUNNEL
LANDUNGSBRUECKEN WITH THE OLD ELBETUNNEL

MUSEUMSSCHIFF CAP SAN DIEGO
MUSEUM SHIP CAP SAN DIEGO

FISCHAUKTIONSHALLE AM FISCHMARKT
FISH AUCTION HALL AT THE FISHMARKT

MS EUROPA IM TROCKENDOCK VON BLOHM UND VOSS
MS EUROPA IN DRY DOCK AT BLOHM UND VOSS

HAMBURGS HAFENCITY
AUS ANDERER PERSPEKTIVE
HAMBURG'S "HAFENCITY"
FROM A DIFFERENT PERSPECTIVE

INNENSTADT MIT DER BINNENALSTER
CITY CENTRE WITH INNER ALSTER LAKE

HAMBURGER „MICHEL“ (ST. MICHAELIS)
HAMBURGE “MICHEL” (ST. MICHAELIS)

DER TURM DES HAMBURGER „MICHEL“
IST EIN TOURISTENMAGNET
THE TOWER OF THE HAMBURGE “MICHEL”
IS A MAGNET FOR TOURISTS

DACHBAUARBEITEN
AUF DER ELBPHILHARMONIE
ROOFING WORK ON THE ELBPHILHARMONIE

ARBEITER AUF DER ELBPHILHARMONIE
WORKERS ON THE ELBPHILHARMONIE

ALTER ELBPARK
OLD ELBE PARK

BISMARCK-DENKMAL IM ALTEN ELBPARK
BISMARCK MEMORIAL IN THE OLD ELBE PARK

HAMBURG: VOLKSPARK
HAMBURG: VOLKSPARK

MESSEHALLEN MIT DEM FERNSEHTURM
"MESSEHALLEN" CONFERENCE CENTRE WITH TELEVISION TOWER

HAMBURGER RATHAUS
HAMBURG CITY HALL

HAMBURGS „TANZENDE TÜRME“ MIT ARCOTEL HOTEL
HAMBURG'S “DANCING TOWERS” WITH ARCOTEL HOTEL

HAMBURGER DOM AUF DEM HEILIGENGEISTFELD
HAMBURG "DOM" FAIRGROUND AT HEILIGENGEISTFELD

JUNGFERNSTIEG MIT ANLEGER FÜR DIE ALSTERSCHIFFE
JUNGFERNSTIEG WITH JETTIES FOR THE ALSTER SHIPS

HAMBURGS BINNENALSTER
HAMBURG'S INNER ALSTER LAKE

ALSTERFONTÄNE MIT RUDERBOOT
ALSTER FOUNTAIN WITH ROWING BOAT

ROTHENBAUM - DAS GRÖSSTE TENNISSTADION DEUTSCHLANDS
ROTHENBAUM - THE BIGGEST TENNIS STADIUM IN GERMANY

DAS HSV-STADION
THE HSV STADIUM

ZÜGE IM „MASCHEN RANGIERBAHNHOF“
TRAINS IN “MASCHEN RANGIERBAHNHOF” (MASCHEN RAILWAY YARD)

MASCHEN RANGIERBAHNHOF – DER ZWEITGRÖSSTE RANGIERBAHNHOF DER WELT
MASCHEN RAILWAY YARD – THE SECOND LARGEST MARSHALLING YARD IN THE WORLD

BÜSUMER HAFEN MIT DER GRÖSSTEN KRABBENKUTTERFLOTTE DEUTSCHLANDS
BUESUM HARBOUR WITH THE LARGEST SHRIMP VESSEL FLEET IN GERMANY

NORDFRIESISCHE KÜSTE

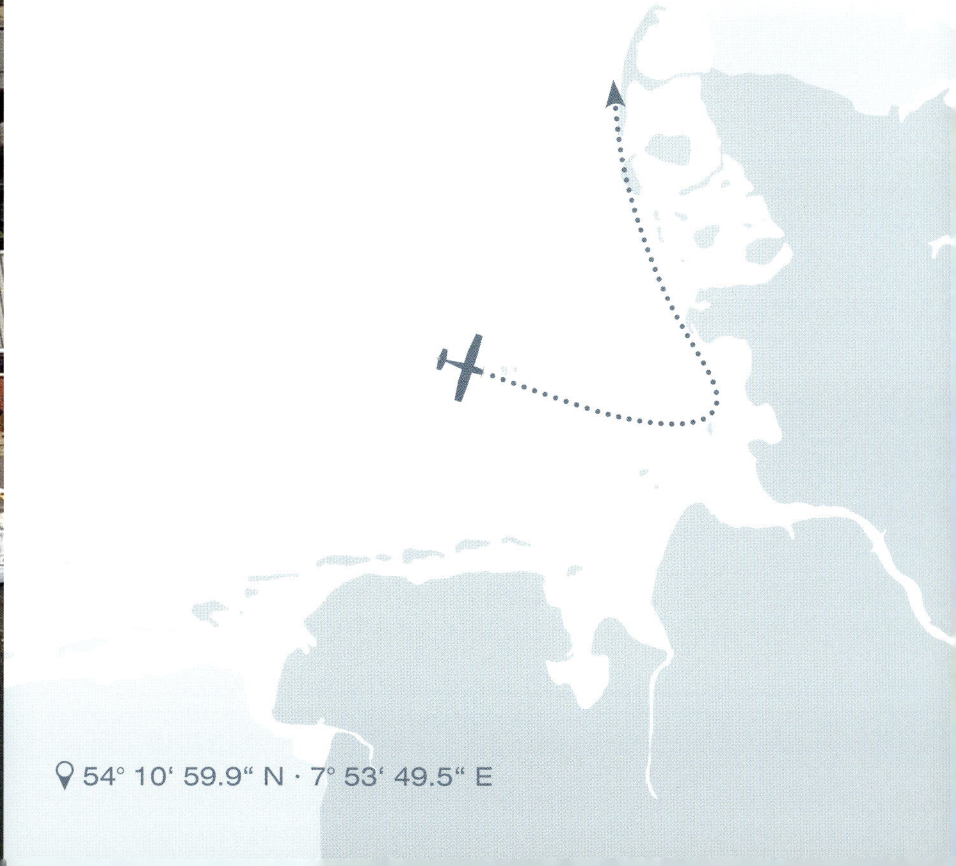

54° 10‘ 59.9“ N · 7° 53‘ 49.5“ E

HELGOLAND -
DEUTSCHLANDS EINZIGE HOCHSEEINSEL
HELGOLAND –
GERMANY'S ONLY ISLAND IN THE OPEN SEAS

DIE LANGE ANNA – DAS WAHRZEICHEN HELGOLANDS
THE "LANGE ANNA" – HELGOLAND'S LANDMARK

HELGOLANDS DÜNE
HELGOLAND'S DUNE

VOR HELGOLAND: AUSFLUGSSCHIFFE BOOTEN TAGESTOURISTEN AUS
OFF THE COAST OF HELGOLAND: TOURIST EXCURSION SHIPS

RESTAURANT AUF DER DÜNE
RESTAURANT IN THE DUNE

HELGOLAND MIT DEM OBERLAND, MITTELLAND UND UNTERLAND
HELGOLAND WITH UPLAND, MIDLAND AND LOWLAND

HELGOLANDS DÜNE HAT EINEN STRAND
UND EINEN KLEINEN LANDEPLATZ
HELGOLAND'S DUNE HAS A BEACH
AND A SMALL LANDING PLATFORM

BÜSUM AN DER NORDFRIESISCHEN KÜSTE
BUESUM ON THE NORTH FRIESIAN COAST

BÜSUMS STRANDPROMENADE MIT SCHWIMMBAD
BUESUM'S BEACH PROMENADE WITH SWIMMING POOL

BÜSUMER HAFEN MIT DEN LEGENDÄREN KRABBENKUTTERN
BUESUM PORT WITH THE LEGENDARY SHRIMP VESSELS

EIDERSPERRWERK MIT SCHLEUSE
EIDER BARRAGE WITH SLUICES

EIDERSPERRWERK AUS ANDERER PERSPEKTIVE
EIDER BARRAGE FROM A DIFFERENT PERSPECTIVE

WATT AN DER EIDERMÜNDUNG
MUDFLAT AT THE EIDER ESTUARY

ST. PETER-ORDING MIT DEN RIESIGEN SANDSTRÄNDEN
ST. PETER-ORDING WITH IT'S EXPANSIVE SANDY BEACHES

KURGEBIET VON ST. PETER-ORDING
SPA AREA OF ST. PETER-ORDING

PFAHLBAUTEN AM STRAND VON ST. PETER
BUILDINGS ON STILTS ON THE BEACH AT ST. PETER

HOCHWASSERSICHER: STRANDGASTSTÄTTE 54°
SAFE FROM HIGH TIDES: BEACH RESTAURANT 54°

ST. PETER-ORDING – HIER DARF SOGAR AM STRAND GEPARKT WERDEN
ST. PETER-ORDING, WHERE IT IS EVEN ALLOWED TO PARK ON THE BEACH

BEKANNTES MOTIV: WESTERHEVER LEUCHTTURM
FAMILIAR MOTIF: WESTERHEVER LIGHTHOUSE

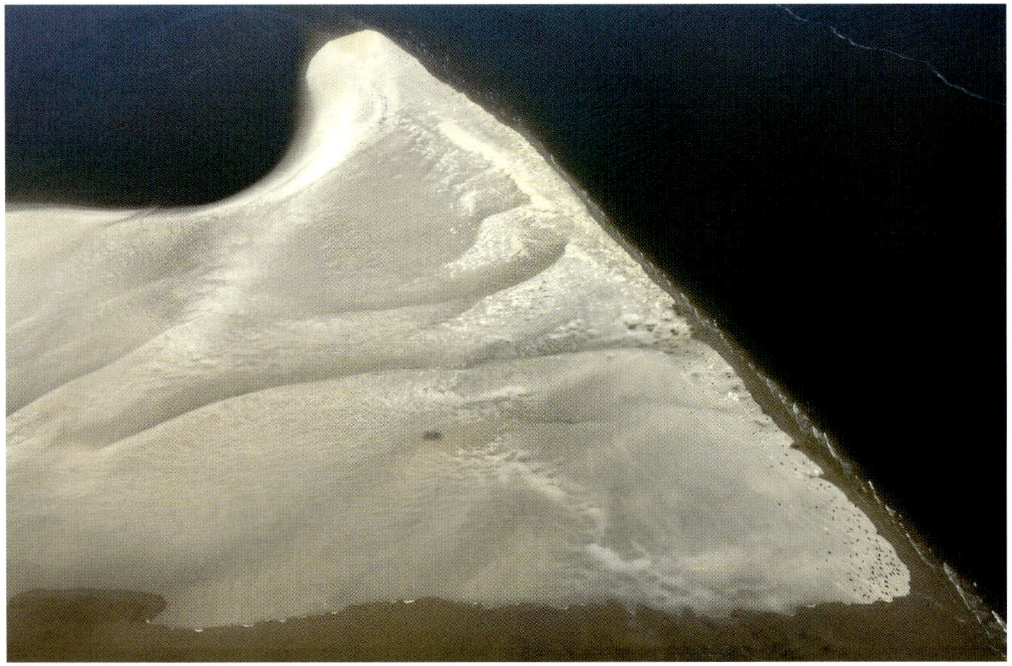

SEEHUNDBÄNKE VOR PELLWORM
SEAL BANKS OFF THE COAST OF PELLWORM

PELLWORM – INSEL IN DER NORDSEE
PELLWORM ISLAND IN THE NORTH SEA

PELLWORM: ALTE KIRCHE
PELLWORM: OLD CHURCH

DIE PELLWORMER LEBEN VON DER LANDWIRTSCHAFT UND VOM TOURISMUS
THE PEOPLE OF PELLWORM LIVE FROM AGRICULTURE AND TOURISM

LANGENESS MAYEN-WARFT
LANGENESS MAYEN WARFT

LANGENESS KIRCHHOF-WARFT
LANGENESS KIRCHHOF WARFT

LANGENESS SPERRWERK „DER JELF“
LANGENESS BARRAGE THE “JELF”

LANGENESS PANORAMA
LANGENESS PANORAMA

HALLIG HOOGE MIT DEM SPERRWERK
UND DER KIRCH-WARFT
HALLIG HOOGE WITH THE BARRAGE
AND THE KIRCH WARFT

HALLIG HOOGE MIT OCKEN-WARFT UND DER HANS-WARFT (HINTEN) UND MITTELTRIFT (RECHTS)
HALLIG HOOGE WITH OCKEN WARFT AND THE HANS WARFT (BEHIND) AND MITTELTRIFT (RIGHT)

WESTER-WARFT AUF DER HALLIG HOOGE
WESTER WARFT ON THE HALLIG HOOGE

FÄHRHAFEN AUF DER HALLIG HOOGE
FERRY PORT ON THE HALLIG HOOGE

HALLIG NORDEROOG – SCHUTZRAUM FÜR VÖGEL
HALLIG NORDEROOG – BIRD SANCTUARY

ANSICHTEN VON HALLIG SÜDEROOG: DIE INSEL WIRD NUR VON ZWEI MENSCHEN BEWOHNT
VIEWS OF THE HALLIG SUEDEROOG: THE ISLAND IS ONLY INHABITED BY TWO PEOPLE

NORDSEEINSEL AMRUM
NORTH SEA ISLAND OF AMRUM

AMRUMS DÜNENLANDSCHAFT
AMRUM'S DUNE LANDSCAPE

AUSFLUGSSCHIFF VOR AMRUM
EXCURSION SHIP OFF THE COAST OF AMRUM

AMRUMER DÜNEN UND NORDDORF (IM HINTERGRUND)
AMRUM DUNES AND NORDDORF (IN THE BACKGROUND)

WITTDÜN AUF AMRUM
WITTDUEN ON AMRUM

DER FÄHRANLEGER VON AMRUM
THE FERRY JETTY ON AMRUM

FÄHRVERBINDUNG VON FÖHR ZUM FESTLAND
FERRY CONNECTION FROM FOEHR TO THE MAINLAND

FÖHR – BELIEBTE TOURISTENINSEL IM NORDEN
FOEHR – WELL-LOVED TOURIST ISLAND IN THE NORTH

FÖHR: DIE ALTE WIKINGER-FESTUNG LEMBERGSBURG
FOEHR: THE OLD VIKING FORTRESS LEMBERGSBURG

DIE STRÄNDE AUF DER INSEL FÖHR
THE BEACHES ON THE ISLAND OF FOEHR

ZENTRALORT WYK AUF FÖHR MIT STRAND UND HAFEN
CENTRAL TOWN WYK ON FOEHR WITH BEACH AND HARBOUR

DIE BERÜHMTE INSEL SYLT
THE FAMOUS ISLAND OF SYLT

LIST AUF SYLT MIT DEM SOGENANNTEN ELLENBOGEN
LIST ON SYLT WITH THE SO-CALLED ELBOW

WESTERLAND BIS LIST
WESTERLAND TO LIST

DER SYLTER ORT MORSUM MIT DEM HINDENBURGDAMM
THE SYLT TOWN OF MORSUM WITH THE HINDENBURG DAM

WESTERLAND AUF SYLT –
ANZIEHUNGSPUNKT FÜR TOURISTEN
WESTERLAND ON SYLT – TOURIST ATTRACTION

SYLT: ANSICHTEN VON KAMPEN (OBEN MIT BLICK INS WATT)
SYLT: VIEWS FROM KAMPEN (ABOVE WITH A VIEW OF THE MUDFLATS)

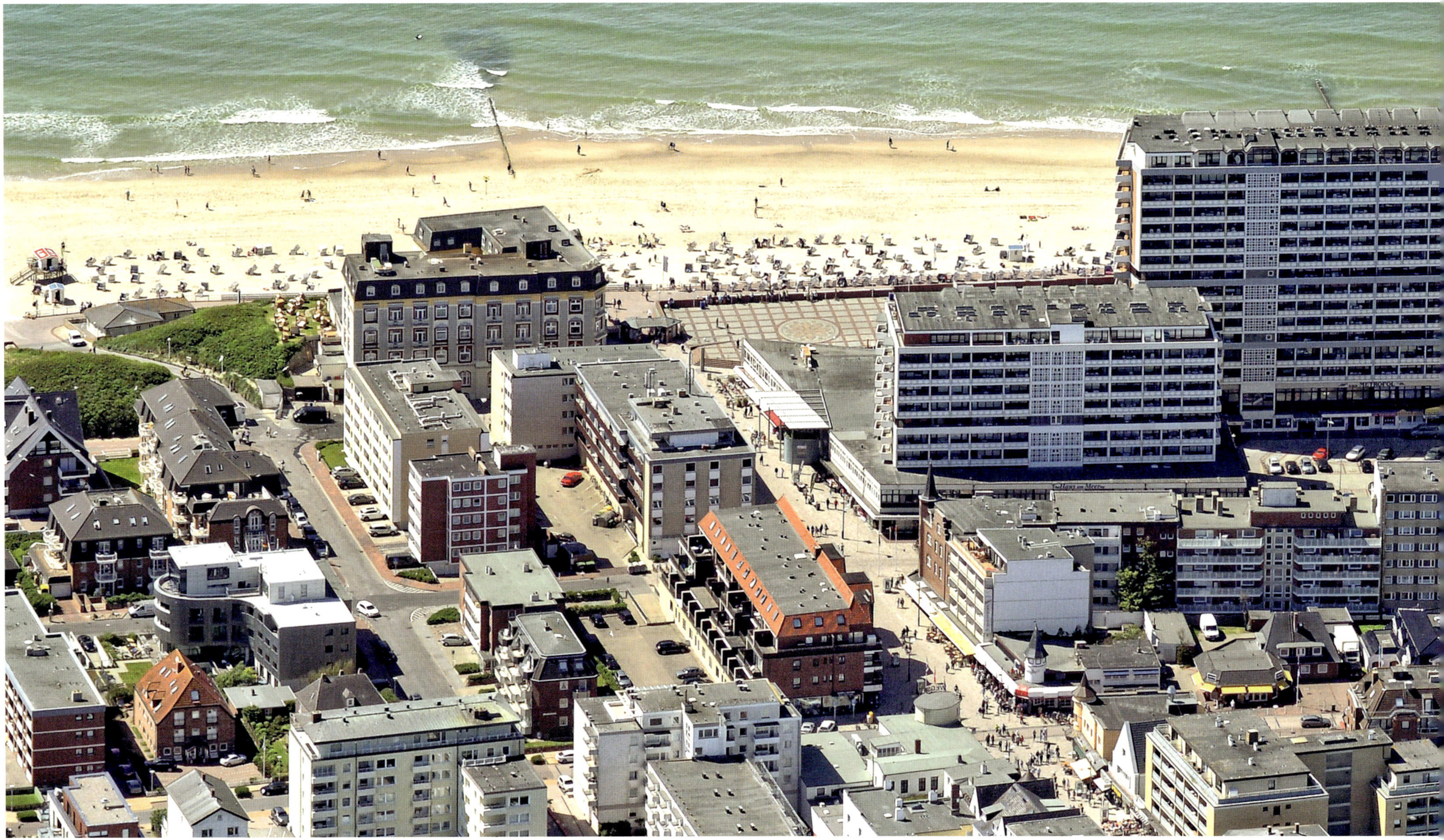

STRANDPROMENADE
BEACH PROMENADE

SYLT MIT HÖRNUMER HAFEN
SYLT WITH HOERNUM HARBOUR

DIE BEKANNTE SYLTER SANSIBAR
THE FAMOUS SYLTER SANSIBAR

ABOUT
MARTIN ELSEN

Das Fotografieren war immer sein großes Hobby – längst ist daraus seine Profession geworden. Martin Elsen arbeitet seit 2006 als freier Fotograf in seiner Heimatstadt Stade. Er fotografiert für die Tourismusverbände der Region, vor allem für viele Firmen, aber auch für Zeitungen wie das Tageblatt in Stade und Buxtehude oder für Fachzeitschriften und andere Publikationen. Ob es um Produktwerbung oder um gekonnte Porträts der Mitarbeiter eines Unternehmens geht – die ganze Palette der Werbefotografie bietet Elsen an.

Sein erstes Geld hat sich Elsen (Jahrgang 1969) schon mit 14 Jahren mit dem Fotografieren verdient, als er auf einer Hochzeit für das Brautpaar Aufnahmen machte. Solche Aufträge nimmt er längst nicht mehr an. Mit zwölf Jahren bekam der kleine Martin seine erste Spiegelreflexkamera geschenkt. Seitdem ließ ihn das Fotografieren nicht mehr los. Im Laufe der Jahre hat der Vater von zwei kleinen Kindern immer mehr an seiner Professionalität gefeilt und sich zunehmend spezialisiert.

Eine dieser Spezialisierungen ist das Fotografieren aus der Luft. Mit seiner hoch auflösenden Spezialkamera hat Elsen von oben fast ganz Norddeutschland fotografiert – und natürlich besonders intensiv seine Heimatregion an der Unterelbe. Mit dem vorliegenden Bildband werden Elsens Luftfotos – viele zeigen besondere Details – erstmals in einem Buch veröffentlicht.

Martin Elsen bedankt sich ausdrücklich bei den Sportpiloten des Stader Luftsportvereins Günther Groenhoff für die Unterstützung. Denn sie bieten ihm mehrmals im Jahr Gelegenheit, in die Luft zu gehen und sein riesiges Luftbildarchiv zu aktualisieren und zu ergänzen.

Photography has always been his favourite hobby – of which he has long made a profession. Martin Elsen has worked as a freelance photographer in his hometown of Stade since 2006. He has taken photographs for the region's tourist associations and above all for many companies, but also for newspapers such as the Tageblatt in Stade and Buxtehude and for specialist magazines and other publications. Whether for product advertising or masterful portraits of company employees, Elsen offers the entire range of publicity photography.

Elsen (born 1969) first earned money for his photography at the age of 14 by taking photos of the bridal couple at a wedding. He has not taken on such commissions in a long while. At the age of twelve, the young Martin received a gift of his first reflex camera. Photography has had him in its grasp ever since. The father of two small children continued to hone his craft and become more and more specialised down through the years.

One of these specialities is photographing from the air. With his special high-resolution camera, Elsen has photographed almost all of northern Germany from above – and of course his home region on the lower Elbe particularly intensively. Elsen's aerial photos, some of which show very special details, have been published for the first time in book format in this collection.

Martin Elsen offers sincere thanks to the sport pilots from the Stader Luftsportverein (air sport club) Günther Groenhoff for their support and for giving him the opportunity, several times per year, to update and add to his enormous aerial photo archive.

Nikon GP-1

www.luftbild.fotograf.de

TRAUMFOTOS ZUM BESTELLEN

Faszinierende Bilder von vielen Regionen Norddeutschlands gibt es im Onlineshop: www.luftbild.fotograf.de

Einfach bestellen und Luftbild oder Landschaftsbild als Download, als Leinwand oder aus hochwertigem Fotopapier in Wunschgröße zuschicken lassen.

Sie wollen mehr als ein Bild in Top Qualität fürs Wohnzimmer oder für ihre Ferienwohnung? Beim virtuellen Rundgang durch das digitale Archiv von Photographie Martin Elsen locken z. B. Helgoland, Cuxhaven und der Landkreis Stade mit inspirierenden Natur- und Landschaftsaufnahmen nicht nur aus der Luft.

Fascinating photographs of many regions of Northern Germany are available from the online shop: www.luftbild.fotograf.de

Simply order and have your aerial photo or landscape photo sent to you as a download, canvass or on high-quality photo paper, in your desired size.

Would you like more than one top quality photograph for your living room or holiday home? The virtual tour of Martin Elsen's digital archive lures with inspiring nature and landscape photographs, for example, of Helgoland, Cuxhaven and the district of Stade not only from the air.

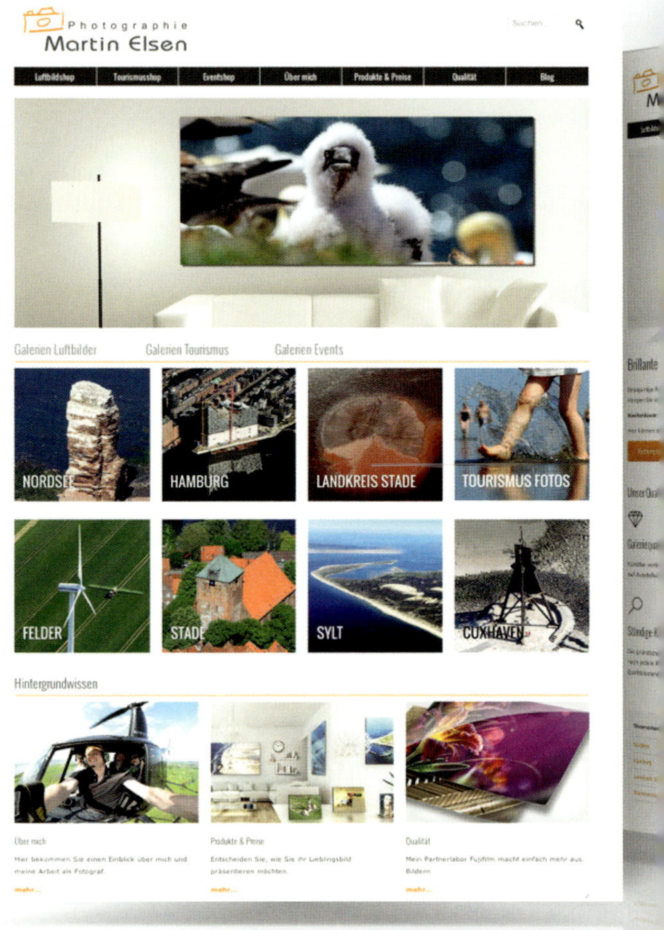

www.luftbild.fotograf.de

Christian Wüstenberg · Silke Schranz

DIE NORDSEE VON OBEN
DIE OSTSEE VON OBEN

Als der aus Otterndorf an der Elbe stammende Filmemacher Christian Wüstenberg Luftbilder seiner wunderschönen Heimat gesehen hatte, war er so sehr fasziniert, dass er gemeinsam mit seiner Freundin Silke Schranz die Idee hatte, einen abendfüllenden Kinofilm über die Nordsee und ihre Küsten aus der Vogelperspektive zu machen. So entstand ein Film, der überwältigende Luftaufnahmen vom Weltnaturerbe Wattenmeer zeigt, von den Inseln und Halligen und vom Land hinter dem Deich. Die filmische Reise beginnt in Ostfriesland entlang der Küste und geht hoch bis nach Sylt – ganz ähnlich wie in diesem Buch.

Auch von den Fotos von Martin Elsen war Wüstenberg sofort begeistert und empfindet die Bilder als hervorragende Ergänzung zu seinem Film.

www.die-nordsee-von-oben.de
www.die-ostsee-von-oben.de

As film-maker Christian Wüstenberg, originally from Otterndorf at the river Elbe, saw aerial photographs of his home, he was so fascinated that he and his girlfriend Silke Schranz were inspired to make an evening-long film about the North Sea and its coasts from above. The result is a film of overwhelming aerial views of the World Heritage Site, Wadden Sea, of the islands and "Halligen" as well as the landscape behind the dike. The motion picture journey begins in East Friesia along the coast and continues north to Sylt – very similarly to this book.

Wüstenberg was also immediately thrilled by Martin Elsen's photographs and sees the photographs as an excellent complement to his film.

www.die-nordsee-von-oben.de
www.die-ostsee-von-oben.de

Trailer · Youtube